Sweet HARVEST

PATHFINDER EDITION

By Dana Jensen and Adele Conover

CONTENTS

Nature's C

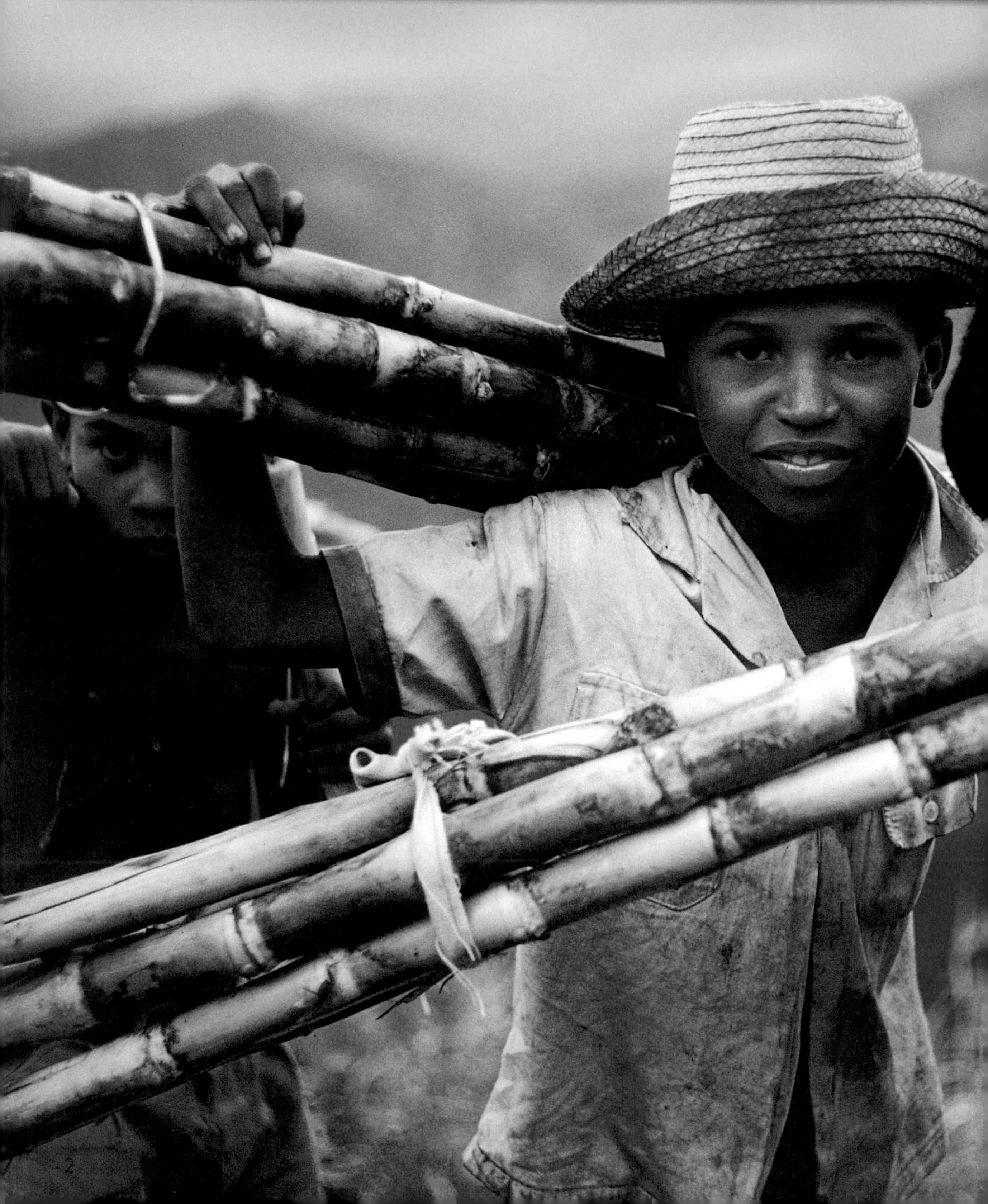

ndy

By Dana Jensen

W ho doesn't love a sweet treat? The sweeter, the better, right? It seems that we put sugar in everything these days. Think of soda, candy, juice, and the crunchy cereal you eat in the morning before school. Sugar is added to all of those things to make them as yummy as possible.

Did you ever stop and wonder where sugar came from? Probably not. Take a look at the picture on the left. What could it possibly have to do with sugar? Step into nature's candy shop to find out.

Popular Plant

Those stalks in the photo may look like bamboo. They are not. They are actually a plant called sugarcane. It just might be the world's most popular plant. That's because almost all the sugar used today comes from this sweet plant.

Sugarcane is a tough plant to grow. It needs lots of water, soil rich in helpful chemicals, and plenty of bright sunshine.

Sugarcane can take anywhere from 8 to 22 months to **ripen**. As the thick stalk grows taller, the juice inside grows sweeter. The juice is at its sweetest when the cane is fully ripe. At that point, the plant is ready to be picked.

Workers slash down the ripe sugarcane stalks. Machines crush them to squeeze out every last drop of the sweet juice. Next, the juice boils in large pots until it turns into a thick, sticky mass of grains and syrup.

Machines then separate the tiny grains from the syrup. Those little grains pack big sweetness. They are sugar grains.

Chew on This!

Sugar isn't the only treat to come out of nature's candy shop. Next, let's look at the trees. People have been chomping on parts of some trees for thousands of years. Sounds odd, doesn't it?

When the bark of a tree is sliced, it produces **sap**, a sticky fluid, to patch itself. When the sap dries, it forms a rubbery blob. People learned long ago that the sap of some trees is perfect for chewing. Native Americans chomped on sap from spruce trees. Greeks gnawed on sap from mastic trees. Ancient Maya chewed the sap of sapodilla trees.

Gum is a bit different now than it was then. People have added sugar for sweetness. Flavors, like mint, vanilla, or fruit, give gum yummy tastes. Gum now comes in all shapes, sizes, and colors. But remember: No matter how much gum has changed, our bubble-blowing habits all started with tree sap.

The Chocolate Tree

Like gum, chocolate also begins in the trees. It comes from the seeds, or beans, of tropical cacao (kuh KOW) trees. Workers cut the bright yellow **pods**, or fruit, off the cacao tree. Next, they crack the pods open and scrape the beans out.

The beans then sit in huge bins for several days. The insides of the beans start to change. That gives them their chocolaty taste. Finally, the beans are roasted and ground into powder.

People long ago mixed chocolate powder with water and drank it. The bitter drink tasted nothing like the chocolate that we eat now. The taste that we love today comes from adding sugar, milk, and other ingredients. Despite those added flavors, however, we still have the cacao tree to thank for chocolate.

Next time you bite into candy, gum, or chocolate, remember where it came from. As you now know, nature can be pretty sweet.

Sweet Job. *A worker plucks pods from a cacao tree in Malaysia. Workers will then open each pod and take out the beans.*

4

Sticky Business

These workers in Mexico make gum the traditional way—by hand.

Drip. A worker slashes a tree, and gooey sap pours out. The sap will become gum.

Strain. Workers pour the milk-colored sap through a strainer to remove dirt.

Stretch. A worker stirs the sap until it is as stretchy as taffy. It turns into gum.

Squeeze. A worker shoves the gum into a box. Workers will then cut the gum into pieces.

From Bean to Bar

Chocolate starts as the seeds, or beans, of the cacao pod. But the raw beans are not very tasty. Here's a look at the many steps it takes today to turn the bitter beans into a yummy chocolate bar.

1 First, you pick the cacao pods and take out the raw seeds, or beans.

2 You let the beans ferment, or change. Then you dry the beans.

3 Then you roast the beans and break them up. This makes cacao nibs.

4 Next, you grind up the nibs. This makes cacao paste.

5 Once you have cacao paste, you add sugar to make chocolate. Or you press the paste to make cocoa butter and cocoa powder.

6 Now, you are ready to make milk chocolate. Mix the cocoa butter and cocoa powder with milk and sugar.

7 Finally, you shape the mixture into chocolate bars.

Cool Beans. *Chocolate is made from the seeds inside a cacao pod.*

PASS THE CHOCOLATE

By Adele Conover

Don't be surprised if one day your mother says, "Eat your chocolate. It's good for you." Scientists have discovered that chocolate is good for your body. It has stuff found in some **vitamins**. Take out the sugar and fat from chocolate bars. What is left is good for your heart and blood.

Scientists now know that some of the stuff in chocolate acts like vitamin C. Vitamin C is good for you. It "grabs" onto harmful things in your body. It keeps the harmful things from hurting your body's organs. It also keeps your arteries from being clogged. Arteries are vessels that carry blood away from the heart. Some of the stuff in chocolate may even fight cancer. But no one knows for sure. The research is not finished yet.

Bitter Beginnings

The first chocolate product was developed thousands of years ago. It did not have sugar. It began with a few small cacao trees growing wild in Central American rain forests. Scientists think Native Americans saw an animal, perhaps a monkey, grab a cacao pod off the trunk of a small tree. The pod was yellow or red. It looked like a small football with ridges. The animal probably ripped open the pod's tough shell. Then it gulped down the white fruit inside. As it ate the fruit, purple-black beans, or seeds, fell onto the forest floor.

Eventually humans figured out how to use the seeds for food. First they ground the seeds into a powder. Next, they mixed the powder with hot water. Then they cooled it to make a chocolate drink. The drink was bitter. They spiced it with vanilla and chili peppers!

The First Chocolate Lovers

Most scientists believe the first people to make this type of chocolate drink were the Olmec. They lived about 3,000 years ago on the coast of Central America.

Making the Cut. *A worker uses a big knife to hack off a cacao pod.*

Spill the Beans. *This open pod is still green, but it will turn red or yellow when ripe. White fruit covers its dark seeds.*

The Medicine Drink

Around 600 C.E., the ancient Maya raised cacao trees in parts of what are now Mexico and Guatemala. Only men were allowed to enjoy the chocolate drink. They took it to cure stomachaches. They drank chocolate to give them strength. They used it to get well from diseases.

The Aztec came into power in central Mexico in the late 1300s. They called their chocolate drink *xocoatl* (shoh KOH hat). It was only for very important men. Like the Maya, they also took it as medicine. The Aztec considered cacao seeds very valuable. They even used them for money.

Chocolate Goes to Spain

In 1519, the Aztec king Moctezuma served Spanish explorer Hernán Cortés some *xocoatl*. Cortés wrote to the king of Spain. He said that the drink tasted bitter, but "a cup of this precious drink permits a man to walk a whole day without food."

In 1528, after Cortés conquered Mexico, he sailed to Spain with cacao seeds. He introduced *xocoatl* to Spain. Then, to sweeten the taste, the Spanish added sugar to their "chocolate." They kept the recipe a secret, though. It took more than 80 years for the rest of Europe to learn how to make the drink. When other Europeans did catch on, a chocolate craze spread across the continent.

THE STORY OF CHOCOLATE

1000 B.C.E. People called the Olmec raise cacao trees in Central America.

600 C.E. The Maya use cacao seeds to make a chocolate drink.

1519 Moctezuma offers a chocolate drink called *xocoatl* to Hernán Cortés.

1528 Cortés takes *xocoatl* to Spain. He teaches the Spaniards how to make it. They heat it. They add sugar. They keep the recipe a secret.

1600s The rest of Europe learns the secret.

Main Squeeze. *Smooth chocolate is squeezed out of this machine, just like toothpaste from a tube. The bar shapes harden quickly.*

Junk Food or Health Food?

In the early 1700s, a Dutch chocolate maker invented a machine to press chocolate into a "cake." These cakes eventually evolved into something like our candy bars.

Today, scientists and chocolate makers are working to make chocolate products that are lower in fat and sugar. If they succeed, you might have to think twice about calling candy bars junk food.

WORDWISE

pod: a container for seeds that grows on some plants

ripen: to become ready to eat

sap: sticky liquid inside a plant

vitamin: something in food you need to stay healthy

1657 A shop in England sells solid chocolate to be made into a drink. Chocolate houses soon appear throughout Europe.

1700s The English add milk to their hot chocolate drink.

1765 The first U.S. chocolate factory is built.

1900 U.S. chocolate makers use a milk chocolate recipe to make candy bars.

2010s The average American eats 12 pounds of chocolate a year.

Sweet Endings

Bite into nature's sweet treats to answer these questions.

1 What does sugarcane need to grow? How long does sugarcane take to ripen?

2 What two kinds of candy are made from trees? What parts of a tree are they made from?

3 What is the traditional way to make gum? List the steps.

4 What people ate chocolate first? How did they prepare it?

5 What events have changed the way people eat chocolate? How are the events related?